Copyright © 2020 by Letha Goodman

All rights reserved. This book or any portion thereof may not be reproduced or used in any manner whatsoever without the express written permission of the publisher except for the use of brief quotations in a book review.

Printed in the United States of America

ISBN 978-1-7356884-0-4

TABLE OF CONTENTS

Introduction 2
Aspire Mental Freedom 4
My Confession 7
Prayer Time 8
Dear God 10
Mama I Am Sorry 14
Dear Children, I Am Sorry 16
To My Family 18
My First Main Pain 21
My Drive To Love Even Harder 24
Thorns In My Side 27
People Who Could Help Chose Not To 29
To All Mothers 31
Ladies Release The Mental Chains And Free Yourself 35
Being Constantly Reminded Of What More I Need To Do 37
Dear Self 39

MOTIVATION OF LIFESTYLE CHANGE

Elevate your life by elevating your mind

It's okay to free yourself, but allow life's lessons to humble you

Doubt your doubts but don't doubt God

You are greater than your circumstances

Start right now by renewing your mind and

Give yourself a greater chance

INTRODUCTION

It is very hard forcing yourself to do right, especially when you have spent a lot of your life doing wrong or being wrong in the eyes of others. The pressure and the anxiety that comes with trying and praying, and praying and trying, can weigh you down. Some people actually get to a point in life when what is not happening matters. Truthfully speaking, there are a lot of people who have done foolish and bad things over and over again, but not because they decided one day they were going to be a bad apple, people just tend to make stupid, foolish, selfish decisions with no valid reason why.

Life for me has been an ongoing challenge. As you read, I ask that you keep in mind this is a peep into my life, my flaws, and also things that I have been longing for. This is not an attack, this is just me expressing myself in a way that I have been wanting to do for years. Through my expressions, I truly want to help and inspire people. So, to get the complete understanding you must read this until the end with an open mind.

I am learning more and more that as we live each day of our lives, we should strive to take each day as a blessing and a lesson. The way our lives are constantly viewed and critiqued by others will always be analyzed, as if we are living under the microscope. We tend to carry on our day-to-day actions of our day-to-day living the way we want others to see us at times. This is a challenge for a lot of people and a struggle for most. Some people, such as myself, from time to time have put on this way of doing what can be done in those moments to portray themselves the way they want people to view them and their family at that moment. I am here to tell everyone this is not how things should be done at all. The major problem with this is we have no business trying to live behind a mask for people to view us or our family a certain way and that we should be more concerned about pleasing God. We should be more concerned about how we are living out loud in front of God. In actuality, I had to learn over time that I first needed to put more energy into me creating the world I wanted to live myself, no matter how far-fetched it seemed at those times or in those moments.

ASPIRE MENTAL FREEDOM

Dreams and aspirations: what are they? As a child, there are a lot of things, crazy things that I can remember about myself. I have always talked to myself. Times when I was by myself, I used to pretend that I was preaching to a crowd of people. Writing was also something I have always done. Running my mouth has always been the norm. Creative writing, poetry writing, extemporaneous writing, sermon preparation, and biographies, for the most part, seem to always be a good form of escape for me. When I write prayers, or thoughts, or whatever, I tend to feel free. It has taken years for me to finally complete this project and do all I can in this particular work to help and heal as many people as possible, starting first with myself. This book is based off some of my experiences and my mindset of how I view things. This book is medicine for me, and I hope for you also.

There are a lot of things in life that I have faltered on. There were even times I faltered so much that I felt broken beyond repair, low, of no value, lonely, helpless and hopeless. For me now, especially my mental well being, I need to free myself. I have a habit of always talking and not letting others talk. I have a habit of not giving others respect at times, or the space they deserve to allow them to finish what they are saying. This is mainly because I either don't want to hear what they have to say, or I just don't want to hear it at all. This book is to bring focus and attention to some things that many of us have encountered, or are presently encountering, and is a cry for all of us to reflect more on the things that are important: family, love, togetherness, empathy, respect, communication, understanding, insight, support, redirection, purification and most of all, God. I am a believer that God should always be on our minds and in our actions, no matter what.

This writing is strictly about me and some things I feel that I have not been able to say. I don't blame anyone, because I have made it hard for people to listen to me, mainly because I have failed to listen to them. I want to take this moment to thank all the positive, inspiring people who accepted me in spite of it all. You have all nurtured me, you have all mentored me and loved on me, you have all taught me and held my hand along the way. I have been able to cry on your shoulders. I have been able to call and vent some of my frustrations to you. I want to thank all of your right now, in this moment. I also want to thank everyone who is reading this book. Right now, I ask for you to free your mind and do your best to feel what is inscribed on these pages.

#MOTIVATIONOFLIFESTYLECHANGE

THINGS MAY BOTHER YOU, BUT THEY DON'T HAVE TO DEFEAT YOU

PRESS BEYOND THE HARDSHIP, AND FOCUS ON PERSEVERANCE

MY CONFESSION

I have asked God a lot for abundance of financial blessings when instead I should have been praying more for abundance of family restoration. I have asked God a lot to bless me when I should have been praying more to bless the togetherness of my family. I have asked God a lot to give me the desires of my heart when I should have been praying more for God to shape my mind to live for God's heart. I have asked God a lot to bless my ministry when I should have been praying more for God to minister to my family. I have asked God a lot for the provisions for a bigger house when I should have been praying more for God to be the centerpiece of my home. I have asked God a lot to allow me peace and joy when I should have been praying more for my family to be full of love, loyalty, joy, and happiness. The more I read, study, and pray, the more I realize that my mindset is constantly shifting.

PRAYER TIME

Heavenly Father, I come to you right now claiming victory for anyone reading this prayer, bringing remembrance of hope for this day of joy. Lord, guide us in patience and understanding for our jobs, homes, friendships, those we associate with, relationships, and ministries. The ability You have to elevate is higher than the sky above, it is bigger than the universe, for You can't be measured, which means Your ability to bless is uncontainable, for the blessings on our lives are never-ending. Our missions are great, our ministries are bigger, we are not enslaved by this world. We will appreciate what You give us in the act of saving, not going more into debt, for we claim freedom from debt, our finances are unmeasurable, for we are the lenders and not the borrowers, we are the blessers of those who are less fortunate, our men are able to be saved regardless of what the world may say, our children are of Your royal priesthood, we are united not by race, color, creed, or denomination, but by faith that You are creator and Jesus died so that we may be free. We decree that nothing, no one, no lie, no illusion will separate us from You. There is healing physically, there is healing spiritually, we cast our worries, hurt, pains, frustrations, and agitations to You. We understand we are not worthy. We thank You. We worship You. We will love the unloved, listen to those unheard, and there are none un-churched because we acknowledge that the "One Church" is the people. We bare all on Your alter of grace, in Jesus' name and by the power of His blood......Amen

Dear God,

Fill my family's heart with LOVE, LOVE, LOVE, LOVE, LOVE, LOVE, excitement, and joy for each other. Amen.

DEAR GOD

Dear God, I know You called me, but sometimes the question raises in my mind, why? Yes God, I know that I am to preach The Gospel, however, the thought of why just tends to run a little deeper. Dear God, the thoughts of my mistakes consume the present joy of my happiness, and sometimes I can't help but cry. As my tears pour out quietly like the midnight rain it feels like I am drowning, but You, oh God, have always been my life support. Still, at times, I can't help but wonder: why call a person such as myself whose life is just not where it needs to be? I believe that we all have sinned and fallen short of Your glory; yet sometimes, the thunderstorms of negativity occur in my mind. The mental hurricanes are real. I have thoughts of uncertainty of being in the ministry. I have thoughts of uncertainty when it comes to sharing my story with others. I have thoughts of uncertainty when it comes to people outside of my family, because there are some that I have opened up to who basically vanished in the wind. I have thoughts of rejection. I have thoughts of inadequacy. I have thoughts of traveling this road, especially alone, and it ails my heart, my actions, and my thought process. My God, I just want to do better and love better. God, I want to be more pleasing to You. I want my family to love You and not rebel against You. I truly want us to get back to the basics of Your purposed intention for us being here. Yet it still feels like I can't shake the attacks that come my way or the way of my family. Dear God, show me Your purpose and Your plan. I pray that others, especially those I infinitely love, are able to see the delight in living for You. Thank You for this season, though I don't understand it all.

For some time now, I have been trying to spend extra time with my family and it seems as if that is all that I am doing: trying. I truly cherish my family and I know deep down inside they cherish me as well. I just wish everyone, especially my immediate family, would take into consideration that the time we spend together should not be taken lightly. Every year when my birthday, Thanksgiving, Christmas, New Year's, Valentine's Day, Easter, and Mother's Day roll around, I am always asked: what do you want? All I have been praying for and living for is my family. There is nothing more important to me than those who I hold most dear to my heart. I have moments where I feel left out, not a priority, not acknowledged, or not appreciated in return. It's like I have to have my family. I know for some people that may be selfish, but for me, if I don't have my family then what do I have of value? The more I write or think of my wish list for things I really want to have, I realize the things that I desire to have the most cannot be bought with money. Each day I get older and older and I know for a fact time waits for no one. It is very depressing for me when I see or hear about people losing their family members for whatever reason. I just don't want to take any time for granted. Yes, I want to spend way more time with my family. It would not bother me if we were all under one roof. I just want to spend as much time as possible with my family. I don't understand why people don't make family time a constant priority. Outside of the life that God gave us, He gave us family.

Dear God, one minute my life seems so pleasurable, then boom, the next minute something happens that knocks my focus off course. Please Lord, I pray for the negative thoughts to stop. The enemy is preying against me and everything I love. I want to stay focused. Yet the distractions come. I want to stay the course, though I tend to constantly make mistakes. Many times I have moments that I wonder, should I press forward with what You have called me to do? There are some reflections of my life's past and present that concern me. What will my future be, God? What is in store for me? I want to have more days of sunshine, joy, and peace. I don't want others to be misled or misguided based off what they think they know or see, with no full knowledge or understanding. I must confess, it has taken me over six years to move forward with this book because honestly, I was afraid.

My concerns of how others would view my thought process or the way I see things have disturbed me for far too long. Also, I honestly could not figure out how I was going to be able to financially support this endeavor. Weary and wondering late nights, sometimes all I did was just imagine that one day, this moment right here would be a reality. I would imagine it all throughout the day sometimes. In this moment, I move forward. In this moment, I press forward. In this moment, I pay it forward.

In this moment, I claim that I will continue to humble myself and always be willing to learn. Will I think back? Yes, I will. Will I get it all right? No, I will not. In this I trust and believe that as long as I am doing all I can to be pleasing to You, then You, God, and only You alone, will protect me, lead me, and guide me through. I made a promise to You, God, and I will keep that promise to share my story and my feelings more and more. I realize I do not have to apologize for how I feel. However, I also understand that we all have feelings, and the same way I want others to be considerate of my feelings, I too must be more considerate of their feelings as well, with the deepest sincerity. My hopes, my dreams, and my aspirations are mine and mine alone, so with that being said, I must encourage others to reach the highest height that they can, for they should also have their own hopes, dreams, and aspirations. My main message for myself and others is to humble ourselves before You, God, and to take heed of Your will, Your way and not our own. We are all here to serve You in whatever we do. Our actions should be a reflection of You and not what this world has been force-feeding us to do. I know You have called me. I know that troubles don't last always. I just don't want others to assume that because of my past, it's okay for them to travel down the same path. Please God, I want to stop others from going down a path of darkness. Dear God, please help me help others with this work. Dear God, Thank You.

MAMA I AM SORRY

To my mama, Imodene Bell, I am sorry. Even though time continues to go on and on, my missing you never stops. Thinking about times where you poured your heart into all that you did for your children is so emotionally overwhelming. You worked so hard! You never made excuses as to why something could not get done. You gave us the foundation of the upbringing your parents gave you, and for that I am ever grateful. I still cry, because in my mind, if you were here, life for me would be so much easier. I know this is selfish and the sad part is that I did not appreciate you enough while you were here. Hate is a strong word, but I hate the fact that while you were here, I caused you many tears and pain. I am sorry for the times I embarrassed you. I am sorry for hurting you. I am sorry for not appreciating you. I am sorry for the times of not caring or not taking your feelings into consideration. Mama, I am sorry you constantly gave your all. Mama, I am sorry. I never meant to do the things I did, yet I still did the same things over and over again. Mama, I'm sorry. Down to the depth of my soul my barrenness inside never fails to cry. The emptiness inside I have is yet to be controlled. I just miss you. It seems so unfair, and here I am now crying out to you, screaming to the heavens above with so much despair. Mama, there was so much damage that I caused, and I am sorry for not honoring you. I am sorry that I rebelled against you. I am sorry that at times, I made you feel as if you were not a good enough mother. I am sorry that I did not value you enough when you were here. I know there is nothing I can do to change the past or bring you back, but if I could, I would just want to be in your arms for a little while to tell you, "I love you Mama, you are the best in the world." Oh, how I miss you so. It is hard. The older I get, the harder it seems, because I can't help but think it is because I took God, my family and my salvation for granted. Now, I take all of these things more seriously each and every single day. I would never have imagined that with all the joy, happiness, delight, and smiles that parenthood brings, it also has challenges. For years I have cried those heartbreaking motherly tears. I have experienced the motherly sorrow. I am also sorry for all the wrong I have done even after God called you home. I am sorry that I let you leave here wondering if you failed as a mother. The truth is, you did not fail; I just failed to be obedient to your instructions. I was just too stupid to not pause and embrace your ever-abundant love and instruction for me. There is no excuse for the bad choices I made in my past. I now strive daily to encourage others to be better. I am sorry. Had I known that motherhood would have constant labor pains throughout, I would have appreciated you more.

DEAR CHILDREN, I AM SORRY

To my children, I am sorry. If I could have foreseen that today would be as it is now, I would have done better. I invited you all into a brokenness that is hard to repair and I am sorry. I have neglected you all and not loved you all as a mother should. I do not know why, but I did. I do really love you all. I just want you all to be better than me. You are all so gifted, talented, and funny. I love you all so so much. It was never my intention to be separated from my children. The only person who is truly at fault is me. I have tried to fix the past by forcing unity, togetherness, and prayer. I just wanted my family. I have taken a lot of things for granted over the years. The most valuable thing I have taken for granted has been time. When I was younger, I treated time as if I would always have tomorrow, and I realized that tomorrow never comes. I know I get on your nerves, but honestly, I just want the best for all of you. I pray for you all daily. I pray that God continues to protect you all and to cover you. I pray that you all are away from hurt, harm, and danger. I pray that God comforts you all, especially when we are apart. I am sorry for not being who you all have truly needed me to be from day one. I love you all. I am sorry. A mother is supposed to protect her children. I feel as though I have pre-exposed you all to things that have caused you all to believe anything and everything is okay. But, not everything is okay. Not everything is acceptable. The type of company you keep does matter. You should not be friends with everyone. Yes, I learn as I go, and I pray that you all understand that you motivate me to want to be better. As time continues, just understand that everyday should be day greater. Do not settle.

To my princess, my beautiful daughter: I love you. You are so precious! Be the young woman and the royal queen that God wants you to be. Show God how thankful you are to Him for blessing you with the gifts and talents that He has given you. To my wonderful sons: carry yourselves with dignity and pride. Do not allow yourselves to speak in an uneducated manner or you will not sound intelligent. You both are so much better than that. Pray constantly to God. Be men after God's heart. Strive more and more each day to live for God. Carry yourselves as gentlemen. Treat people, especially women, the way you want people to treat your mother. To all of my children: when I am not with you all, my heart misses beats. I do not delight in being away from you all, but I am delighted that you are my children.

TO MY FAMILY

To my hardest critic and the person who has always supported each and every endeavor I have ventured out to do, thank you. Thank you for constantly showing me and reminding me that this world cannot limit my success. I know over the years I have not supported you in your dreams, and for that, I am sorry. I have learned that one of the worst things to do to anyone is not support them or make them feel bad about their dreams and aspirations when all they have done was support yours. Thank you for constantly reminding me that we are all entitled to our own mistakes and that we should not try and force how we think others should live on other people. Thank you for the consistency of your unwavering support. There were so many times that I wallowed in my self-pity and you listened; however, you also always reminded me to do something about it. Even in the moments that I felt overwhelmed about my career choice or my job, you constantly reminded me how beneficial it was for me to be able to be in the presence of the person that I worked for because of his level of success over the years. You reminded me that everything is not about money especially when it involved me learning, training and taking classes because those things would only help me. You helped inspire me with confidence to learn about business because it would only contribute to the progress of my growth. Thank you.

To my grandparents, both paternal and maternal (rest in Heaven), my parents, my siblings, my nieces, my nephews, my aunts, my uncles, and my cousins, my spiritual mom, my best friends, my spiritual family, my church, my supporters in ministry, all of my advisors, I am sorry. I promise I will continue do my best now to make you all proud of me. I want you all to see that your prayers and sacrifices for me are much appreciated. I want to show the world that people can change, and that people do change for the better. People need to know and understand that we must believe that when our loved ones show us they want to do better, and are determined to be greater, that we should support them in love. (Support does not always have to be financial)

To my Aunt (my mother's youngest sister and the youngest out of nine children), thank you for stepping in when Mama died, I am forever grateful. At an early age, you bore a lot of responsibility that put a lot of pressure on you. Thank you. I am sorry that I didn't think about appreciating you more until after I made major mistakes of my own. I want you to know that I am forever grateful for the sacrifices you made on my behalf. I am proud of you and glad that you are part of my life, and even more grateful that you were part of my upbringing.

To my Aunt (my dad's youngest sister and the youngest out of five children), thank you. You and Grandmama were my go-to people. Never would I have imagined to put any of you through the things that I put you through. You have always been there through rain, sleet, snow, and hail. You have been more that an aunt to me, you also have helped majorly in raising my children. You gave me a place to stay and always gave me the benefit of the doubt. You and Grandmama both gave me never-ending chances. Thank you. I appreciate you, and I am forever grateful.

MY FIRST MAIN PAIN

Saturday, October 14, 1995 was a boom in my life. I remember my mother's youngest sister standing over me telling me that my mom did not make it in that car. My mother, my youngest sister, and I were hit head-on by a drunk driver. There is no adequate way to express how I felt then, but now I can say there was numbness. This tragedy will never go away. The pain still lingers. There I was, a teenager in high school, and the person I rebelled against the most, who loved me the most, was gone. There is no way of coping perfectly. When feelings are inside of you as a child or a teenager, freedom is needed to express yourself without any form of hesitation or fault. Now, do not get me wrong, I had a few people that I did confide in, but I never felt the freedom to confide in my family. People need others they can talk to. Now that I am an adult, I realize that the pain that I am still feeling now is hurt that never went away. I have also realized that some pain never stops hurting. I, at times, dwell on not having a mother. I sometimes dwell on what my life would be like now if I still had my mother. I even dwell on the pain more than the progress, which has caused me to be confined as time passes by this thing I call my first main pain, which is not good, since I allowed pain to be the centerpiece of my existence.

As a teenager, I know I bothered the crap out of my mother, and not in a good way. No matter what, she was a parent, and I do not ever recall seeing her give in or give up. Part of my problem was me being upset because she and my father were no longer joined together. My mother worked very hard. She was a nurse and a very caring person. She believed in discipline, too. No child was going to run over her, no matter what. We were not allowed to walk around in public with our hair not combed; heck, she did not allow us to walk around the house with our hair not combed. My brother was not allowed to lay in the house and just watch television on the weekends or through the week. The core structure and values that were instilled in my mother from her parents, she gave to us. All of her children were taught to cook and yes, we had to go to church. I now realize many of my problems with my children—well, one main problem is I have given them too many options. It hurts even more to realize that the structure I was given, I rejected in the early stages of having children, and here I am now doing all I can to enforce what I allowed to be lost.

Holiday time is painful also. In 2007, I officially cooked my first holiday meal all by myself. I learned in that moment that I need to give more energy to my children. I lived years not feeling as if I had a place to call home, mainly because my mother was gone. My brother always made sure he had a house of his own so that his sisters and their children could always have a place to go. I love my dad, stepmother, aunts, uncles, and cousins, but it is hard being around others in their own space, watching them with their grandchildren when we do not have that. I do not have that. So, every day, my goal is to spend as much time with my children in our home as possible. I want them to enjoy the comforts of our home. They have no business thinking that it is okay to be all over the place. They need the structure and nurturing of their mother, regardless.

MY DRIVE TO LOVE EVEN HARDER

I view life as love. I do my best not to skip a day without saying, "Thank you, Lord" or "Thank You, God" or "Lord, I thank you for it".

God has saved me from myself a lot. I am a person who desires attention and who needs to be loved; I need to feel love. I love to feel needed. I love to be acknowledged. However, I traded love a lot in my life for pain. I allowed wrong to become my right, and I tried to justify it. I knew what I was doing, but I didn't care in those moments, or even realize the severity of the outcome. I often found myself around total strangers who saw some good in me, telling me that God will take care of me. Feeling affirmed that I am not a bad person or a horrible mother made me feel worthy. Encouragement started to unfold in the thought process of how I thought about myself and others. I was put in uncomfortable positions by being around people whose lives were similar to mine. For me, that was scary. It was even scarier to know that other people's situations were worse than mine. I was convicted. My mindset became victimized, and I had a pity party. Yes, for years it seemed as if I were either running into a brick wall or in circles. I even gave up at one point.

People say it takes twenty-one days to change habits or to do something differently, but I disagree. For me, all it took was a decision. There is no time limit to be better. Once I decided I needed to do better I fell before God and cried out. There were things that I immediately stopped doing, there were things that I immediately started doing and there were things that took me a while to transform from, and transform to. There are also things presently that I am still pressing my way through. During these times, God sent me on-earth angels. God showed me that He loves me regardless of my faults. I learned that my family never gave up on me. God's love for me was ministered through so many people who would listen to me and tell me it was going to be okay, but not to give up. Don't give up. This pushed me harder to treat people in a kindly fashion, especially those who mistreated me and did me wrong. My drive to love better and harder was God showing me how important it was to love myself. My drive to love even harder, and press harder, was my beautiful children. My drive to love even harder and to press harder was when an enemy looked me in my face and told me I had no business trying to minister or work with youth when I have not been a good mother. My drive to love even harder and press harder was the moment my daddy told me he was proud of me, especially when I know I disappointed him in the past. My drive to love even harder and press harder was when I started to forgive myself even though other people were holding my past up against me. My drive to love even harder and press harder was every time someone blessed me by them allowing God to use them in my life. My drive to love even harder and press even harder is **John 3:16:** *For God so loved the world that He gave His only begotten Son, that whoever believes in Him should not perish but have everlasting life.* My drive to love even harder and press even harder is that I love my family so. God blessed me with my family, and I press forward daily to love them harder and more.

THORNS IN MY SIDE

Evil comes to steal, kill, destroy, and divide. One challenge I have dealt with until now is the need to always defend myself, or explain myself, to evil. It amazes me when I try to have happy thoughts or try to decrease negative thoughts and someone says something or does something negative that pierces my heart down to the core of my feelings. One of the hardest challenges in life is forcing yourself to do good when you're constantly reminded of your past mistakes. You find yourself adjusting to people and to what they want just to keep them at peace. You find yourself not expressing yourself, and you find yourself putting up with a lot of uneasiness, because in your mind, you just want to keep them at peace. Then, you find yourself dealing with inner anxiety, dealing with hurt, dealing with constant pain when all you are doing is what you can mentally in those moments to just keep them at peace. Then, there you go again, questioning yourself as to why you don't treat people the way they treat you. Then, you may even have conversations with yourself about why you can't depend on these very people the way they depend on you.

I have had my moments where I have felt foolish, yet all I can do is keep striving to keep the peace and go along with the flow. The fact of the matter is, you get to a point when you are done allowing other people to break your peace. Once I started reacting more and considering myself instead, it really became a problem. Evil has been a major thorn in my side. No matter how much I adjusted, it was not good enough. No matter how many time I put myself on the back burner, it was not good enough. No matter how many times I constantly gave people the benefit of the doubt, they constantly just took and took, and in the end, it still was not good enough. No matter how many times I made people and everything they wanted a priority by standing in the background, it still was just not good enough.

PEOPLE WHO COULD HELP CHOSE NOT TO

What amazes me now is the fact that people who could have helped, chose not to. The reality of being a childless mother became reality. I refuse to allow myself to believe in a system where there are intentions to divide families. Pained in my past, rejected, and denied a second chance, my voice and my rights felt as though they were being taken away. Some would disagree, but my realities are my realities and they are factual. Living a monitored parental life, being judged and chastised for how I need to raise my children became so overwhelming and demeaning, all I did was just go with everyone's flow. It's amazing that people will say, "Let me know if you need anything," and when did I seek help from them, they either didn't know how to help or they just were not in the position to do what they said they were able to do. My decision-making was stripped. My life had become so uncomfortable to the point that all I could do for days at a time was cry and ask God why. I grew wearier by the day. I had moments where I just wished somebody, anybody, would tell my children, "Your mother loves you all," or "Do what your mother says," or "Cherish your mother."

I have come into contact with a lot of children who may have had strained relationships with their parents, but I would still remind them to honor their parents and that parenthood was not easy. For the most part, it just seems that the way this world has shifted and the way these laws are written, the very system that is supposed to be in place to help the family, has sadly turned into the devil's advocate. To any judge, social worker, or person period, that does not encourage the relationship of children with their mothers: you are a part of the problem also when it comes to these children. It is not best to just put them somewhere else because they don't want to be somewhere or because they feel like they have that decision to make, even though they are children. Now, don't get me wrong, if there has been abuse, then that is understandable. Keep in mind, when these laws were written, when the gavel strikes, when you say kids sometimes need a break: you are also part of the problem. It is very sad how easy it is to allow these families to be broken in this kind of society where family structure should be mandatory. Family is important.

TO ALL MOTHERS

For those mothers who may feel like they are foreigners in their children's lives, I deeply apologize. Though there are no words that can erase the hurt you feel, I want you to know: it is very important to focus more and more on loving yourself, improving yourself, and energizing yourself by giving yourself more positive energy. As you make decisions for the better, it will not make sense to a lot of people, and sometimes it may not make sense to you. You have to stay the course no matter what, and press your way through. From this point, moving forward, it is okay to make progress without fault or shame, because you are a new woman who will never be the same.

When a woman gives birth to a child, there is no forecast to go by when it comes to raising your child. There is no perfect way to be a mom. When you raise your child or children, it is a learning process throughout. One thing I have learned is to never give up on your children. As your children get older, the challenges of being a mother becomes harder and harder. You may find yourself washed out and tired. You may feel that you have hit a brick wall. However, never give up on your children, and never give your children away. For the most part, whenever a child is separated from their mother for whatever reason, it causes major problems for the child. Of course, things get hard and, yes, we all need help, but one of the worst things to occur is a mother being divided from her children. Sometimes, when life gets hard, we tend to look for other alternatives for our children, especially when it is constantly drilled in your head about doing what is in the best interest for the child. You may have found yourself between a rock and a hard place. You may feel trapped and just need a way out. You may have needed to feel free, or a have a break in between the struggles of motherhood and life. Whatever you are feeling, do not release your children. Do not do it. (The only exceptions would be abuse and/or drugs). Please, ladies, that is one hurt that will never go away.

The challenges will keep coming daily. Sometimes you will find yourself living under the pressure of fighting to keep your family together when the family you love and long for appears to be falling apart with no concern. It might appear that everyone is about doing their own thing and finding their own way without any thought, when all you are striving to do is save them from the intentions of the evil forces that the world has plotted against them to sabotage them. Guess what? They do care. Your family doesn't want to see you hurt. The problem is, we expect people to do things exactly the way we do things. We expect them to give the way we give, when all we have been doing is not making ourselves enough of a priority because we have centered so much on our family. It's almost like you have the vision, but you can't make it happen. Then, you find your mental space interrupted because you have given too much authority to others who are determined to do things their own way no matter the consequences or how you feel about it. In some ways, it feels like you are in competition with others when it comes to raising your children and doing all you can to guide your children, especially when others uphold your children or give your children the impression that they don't have to listen to, respect, or honor their parents. The struggle does not get easier along the way for most mothers, and that is because of the way we have allowed ourselves to cope and deal with things mentally as we tend to mentally over-complicate things.

Don't give in and don't give up

Blessings are part of God's promise, so remain prayed up

You will laugh and you will cry

Don't lose focus

Keep God number One

For what He has already given is the ultimate prize

Shout with praise today on and on

Continue to trust God, for your greater unseen is yet to come.

Yours truly

LADIES RELEASE THE MENTAL CHAINS AND FREE YOURSELF

I know what it's like to do all you can in the moment to be better. A lot of us pray, go to church, and are always willing to give a helping hand. Sometimes, when it comes to giving, the problem is that you find yourself constantly giving while others tend not to give back. I have learned to accept the fact that a lot of people, especially those you hold dear or truly love, will not give back to you in the same manner or to the same standard that you give to them, simply because they just don't want to. When people don't want to do something, it is not a priority. It is hurtful, yes and I understand that at times you tend to make your family, ministries, and your jobs your main priority, when the fact of the matter is, this is the problem. God should always be the ultimate priority. You have evaluated your life, your past and present circumstances, yet you wonder: how did you get here? There may be moments when life seems to be too much, and you are worn out from being tough. Just keep in mind that life is not always a breath of fresh air. Keep in mind that we were all created in a different kind of uniqueness and with all of our differences, we have a greater purpose to live and serve. We tend to slow down our freedom when we dwell a lot on our personal mishaps, and we also slow down our freedom when we reflect a lot on what we did not like about our growing up process. The fact of the matter is, we are all different, and we all come from different backgrounds. There are many of us, even at this very moment, who wish our lives held more value, while others wish our lives were just different right now. I am here to tell you that regardless, you are wonderful. It is time to take total control of your freedom. None of us is the same, and all of our dreams and aspirations are different. Now, inhale slowly, and exhale slowly. Repeat after me:

I am free. I love me for me. God blessed the universe with me. I will not allow anyone or anything to interfere with my relationship with God. I will take more time with God daily. I am thankful for my life. I am free. I appreciate myself, my flaws, and my mistakes. I cherish my family. I will respect the words of the wise. I will think and pause before I speak. I will keep achieving. I will strive to have a more positive attitude. I am a lady of integrity. I am a lady of excellence. I will be productive each day of my existence. I will continue to do great things. I am not bound by any thought, any thing, or any one. I release myself right now, in this moment, because I am free. I free myself.

BEING CONSTANTLY REMINDED OF WHAT MORE I NEED TO DO

One hard lesson I am still learning is that it is not my place to fix people. Though I want the best for those I love, it is hard accepting the fact that they will make their own mistakes and that I need to love them and not make them feel isolated. Isolation is not easy. I am constantly being isolated in so many ways. I am the last to know. I feel as if I don't have a voice at all most of the time. The world around me is steadily showing me that I am not at the top of the priority list and it feels like I am only sufficient as long as I am doing what everyone wants me to do. Sadly, my day-to-day living does not even equate to the calling that I know God has for my life and I feel stuck and I do not know what to do. All I do is plan for my family. My world centers around them, whether they realize it or not.

The more I strive to remind my family that they have so much more to offer and that God has so much more in store for them, it's like I am expected to just drop the ball on them. I refuse to accept the fact that I am not supposed to push my family for greatness. I didn't know it was a bad thing to strive to be a better example for your children and no longer drop the ball on them or yourself. Greatness, I thought, should be expected. I thought it was best to always strive to be better. As a woman in my own right, I thought I had to constantly strive to pour as much energy as possible into those I love or those I want to help. Well, time showed me I was incorrect. In my brain, I thought I was only right, no matter what, that I could correct a lot of my wrongs by going far beyond to help people, even if they showed me they didn't want to help themselves. Well, time showed me this drains a lot of energy, and acting on the process is more challenging than I realized.

DEAR SELF

Dear self,

I am proud of you. You are an achiever. No matter what obstacles have come along, you managed to press your way through, and that deserves applause. You challenged yourself to be better. You are awesome. You are a great woman and a wonderful mother. I am thankful for life in its entirety. I am grateful for my children. I am happy that I finally realized that good always prevails. When I look back, I can smile because I am thankful both for the challenging times and the happy times of my life. My understanding of life now is to do what brings me happiness and not allow life to be any more complicated than it needs to be.

Choose happiness.

Hinderances are merely stumbling blocks: all they do is cause delay. In life, whatever occurs, make yourself a priority and choose to be happy. Ladies, you are worth it. You deserve peace, blessings, and an abundance of joy in your life, but you must choose it for yourself. Remember, the universe is a better place because of your existence. Life is healthier, easier, and better when you love yourself enough to choose yourself. Start now and walk in happiness.

www.ingramcontent.com/pod-product-compliance
Lightning Source LLC
Chambersburg PA
CBHW042329150426
43193CB00005B/62